Copyright © Dyer, 1996.
Copyright © Nacson, 1996. — Questions/Concept
First published in 1996 by
Nacson and Sons Pty Ltd.
P.O. Box 515 Brighton Le Sands 2216
Ph: (02) 281 6179 • Fax: (02) 281 2075

ISBN: 0-947266-15-1

All rights reserved. No part of the publication may be reproduced, stored in a retrieval system, or transmitted in any form or by any means, electronic, mechanical, photocopying, recording or otherwise without the prior permission of the copyright owner.

Printed & bound by: *McPherson's Printing Group*
Typesetting & Cover Design by: *Rhett Nacson*
Cover Photo by: *Image Bank*

DYER STRAIGHT

*An enlightening conversation
with the Father of Motivation and*
Leon Nacson

Consider the possibility of totally eradicating your personal history from your consciousness, and simply living in the present moment. You will find a new freedom as you realise that you aren't relying on the way things used to be to define your life today.

Dedication

~ We dedicate this book to our children.

Acknowledgments

~ We would like to thank our buddy Terry Butler, the Prince of Promoters, for continually making both our lives interesting; Shanna Provost; Leigh Robshaw; Wendy Cramer and Rachel Eldred for their part in research and editing.

DYER
STRAIGHT

*Release the idea that
a failed relationship makes
you a failure. There are
no failed relationships.
Every person who enters
and exits your life does so in
a mutual sharing of life's
Divine lessons.*

Table of Contents

~ Preface
~ Introduction
~ Questions & Answers - **1**
~ Index of Questions - **111**

DYER
STRAIGHT

∽

Develop the sense that anything that is destructive to one human is destructive to all. Know that the essence of life force that flows through you flows through everyone. That awareness will give you a loving energy that will help to bring all of us together.

∽

Preface

~ I'll never forget the first time I met Wayne Dyer. I was having breakfast with Stuart Wilde at the Regent Hotel in Sydney when Wayne jogged up to the table. He was covered in sweat and panting. Dressed in a headband, T-shirt and joggers, he had just completed a five-kilometre jog around The Rocks area of inner Sydney. I was later to learn that jogging is his daily discipline no matter where in the world he finds himself.

Thirty minutes later, after he had showered and shaved, he rejoined us. I warmed to him instantly. We had run many stories about Wayne's work in The Planet over the past few years, and I was happy to meet him at last. He laughed when I told him that when his first book, *Your Erroneous Zones*, hit my desk for

Entertain the thought that you remove habits from your life by coaxing them downstairs one step at a time. Try to catch individual toxic thoughts in the moment they are occurring, one moment at a time, and you will be able to achieve the transition from toxic to pure.

review, I immediately had put it in the pile of books on sex. I told him how disappointed I had been when I took it home, looking forward to a very erotic and sensual weekend of reading, only to discover that the book was about self-empowerment and dealing with emotions! Wayne told me I had been just one of many people who had had this misconception, but he was glad that it induced people to pick the book up and read it just the same.

We settled down to talk about the upcoming Australian and New Zealand tour we were all about to embark on. It was a bold move to gather together all the finest speakers in the field of personal growth that we could muster and to put them on the one billing. The tour in 1994 was perhaps the most successful in which I have had the pleasure to be

Keep a journal. In it, describe what offends you about other people. If you can be objective, you will find that what offends you is really a judgement about how others should be behaving. These judgements are that false idea of yourself, convincing you that the world ought to be as you are, rather than as it is.

involved. Over 20,000 people attended the one-day 'Congress 1994' conferences which were convened by The Seminar Company.

What a cast: Louise L. Hay on her first visit to Australia in five years, Marianne Williamson on her first visit, Stuart Wilde, here straight after the release of *Whispering Winds of Change* and Michael Rowland providing a touch of local talent.

In the years before that conference, hundreds of people had written to *The Planet Newspaper* asking questions of Wayne. During the tour many people even tried to get backstage to experience just a little more of his magnanimous energy or to ask him more questions. When we sat down and looked at all the questions that had been directed at him via The Planet, we discovered that many

Curb your need to be right. If you truly want to work on this area of restraining your ego, then simply respond to what someone has said without offering an argument or a piece of advice. As you practice this technique, your ego will fade, and your relationships will improve.

had similar themes. I decided that as I was in a position where I could grab quality time with Wayne away from the stage, I would see to it that our readers and friends had their questions answered, by hook or by crook.

Every time Wayne turned around I was there with my tape recorder, asking 'just one more question'. Sometimes, I think my fervour drove Wayne crazy, but he was really quite tolerant, and happy in the knowledge that there was a higher purpose to it all. I managed to get answers to many pages of questions and felt that I had satisfied the curiosity of most of our readers. At the end of that busy tour of 1994, Wayne had only 45 minutes to get to the airport from the time he said his parting words on stage. To make matters worse, the limousine had gone to the wrong location and was

DYER
STRAIGHT

Remind yourself that every negative thought you have about another is something you are thinking about yourself. Replace these negative thoughts with positive ones, and your self-esteem and self-worth will grow accordingly.

waiting outside of the hotel instead of the convention centre. Wayne had to jog to the limo so he wouldn't miss his plane home to his beloved family. At that stage, I decided that I would try to get him to answer just a few more important questions. What a sight we must have made jogging down Auckland city streets, Wayne looking agitated and me, like a tenacious terrier, with my walkman virtually up his nostril, jogging beside him. But I was determined to get answers to the last few questions because I knew it was going to be another year before I saw him again. Later I chuckled to myself at my tenacity and his patience.

Wayne often talks about the fact that we create our own reality, and I had created a space in time to get the last few answers I desperately needed. We made it to the limo and out to the airport with

DYER
STRAIGHT

Be still and know. These four words will help you get past striving and help you to know the bliss of being here now. When you allow yourself to be still, you will understand the futility of constant striving or chasing after more.

minutes to spare. As Wayne waved goodbye, I knew his thoughts would be focused on returning to his family while mine were on how to get this information into a digestible format for our readers.

At first, my only intention was to publish it in articles, or in publicity and marketing material for future tours. But, as we began to see the depth and extent of the information we had gathered, I realised it was too good to fragment into small pieces. And thus the book was born.

Because it is a smorgasbord of thoughts and ideas straight from Wayne, we called it *Dyer Straight.* It is the result of all the meetings, conversations and workshops that Wayne and I have shared since that first meeting.

Dyer Straight is written from my perspective, from my personal contact with Wayne. However, I hope the way it is pre-

DYER STRAIGHT

Make an attempt to shift your career objectives from self-absorption to a "calling". Use your talents and special interests to fulfil your service with your calling. Your life work will take on a dramatic shift towards abundance, and you will feel that you are "on purpose".

sented will enable you, the reader, to be with us over the many lunches, dinners and seminars we shared together, and to gain insights into the man behind the presenter. Most people receive but an hour of wisdom from Wayne during a one-day seminar, when there is a multitude of ideas from various speakers to integrate. This book will show you that there is so much more to Wayne, both as a man and as a teacher.

There may be thoughts in the book you've heard or read somewhere before, but we decided to leave it all in because it may help you to reconfirm or rediscover concepts important to your journey. It's like watching a good movie again—you pick up so much more the second or third time you watch it.

I hope *Dyer Straight* will serve as a reference tool for you. As a place to where you can go to have questions answered,

You cannot have a better past, so abandon that thought right now. You did what you knew how to do, given the circumstances of your life. Instead of indulging in regrets, let your thoughts remain on love, and let your actions stem from that love.

concepts clarified, or ideas explained. You may also find in these pages a place where you can simply reconfirm, re-centre and find solace from this crazy world of ours where we often seem to take one step forward and two steps back.

Wayne Dyer speaks with wisdom, and he has an innate ability to lift a person's thinking in a few short words. I hope that you find encouragement in these pages, and I hope that through reading this book, you will be uplifted by Wayne's wisdom and understanding as each one of us who calls him The Father of Motivation is.

Returning from a seminar in Brisbane late one night on the tour, I asked Wayne why he travels so many thousands of miles to speak to auditoriums full of strangers. He turned to me in the back seat of the car and said with conviction,

DYER
STRAIGHT

If enough of us shied away from conflict and confrontation, just imagine how much war we could eliminate.

'My purpose is to get people to look at themselves and begin to shift their concepts. Remember, we are not our country, our race or religion. We are eternal spirits. Seeing ourselves as spiritual beings without labels is a way to transform the world and reach a sacred place for all of humanity.'

Leon Nacson

Learn to allow others to work out their difficulties without feeling that you are the only one who can fix things. Your ego is pushing you to intervene, while your higher self wants you to experience peace and harmony. Choose the latter.

Introduction

~ I watched as Wayne completed his meditation backstage. As he walked through the curtains onto the stage to resounding applause, I sat down in the seat he had just vacated. I could hear him speaking.

'I am talking here today about a higher state of awareness. About reaching what Carlos Castenada talked about as the level of impeccability—the highest level of awareness. About the fact that each and every one of us can make our lives the miracles we would like them to be. We need to understand that we have within us something that is much more divine and much more powerful than we've been led to believe by all the well-meaning sponsors that have shown up in our lives...'

DYER
STRAIGHT

Begin to change the vocabulary you use to describe yourself and your expectations. Instead of saying "Maybe", use "Certainly". When you use words that reflect an absence of doubt, you will conduct your life in the same way.

I thought back to my discussion with Wayne earlier, when we talked about how so many people yearned for something more in their lives, and how they have a spiritual thirst that never seems to be sated—even after attending lots of personal growth seminars and workshops. Why do we feel so dehydrated when it comes to our thirst for spiritual awareness?

'You know, Leon,' he said, 'there are different levels of awareness that are available to us, but most of us buy into what I think of as the survival level of awareness. But there's a place we can get to that is much higher than that. There are certain things we have to do in order to be able to realise the words that Jesus spoke in the New Testament when he said through Saint John, "Even the least among you can do all that I have done and even greater things"'.

DYER
STRAIGHT

Avoid exaggerating or changing facts for the purpose of impressing others. Persisting in this practice will just keep you from knowing your higher self, which needs no exaggeration to feel important in the eyes of others.

'I take that personally and literally. Each of us has within us divine capacities to be able to manifest and create virtually anything that we can conceive of in our life, as long as we stay on purpose. Most of us have bought into a set of beliefs and truths that are not available to us, and when these new truths come and knock on the door, we don't know how to open it, even when we want to. Most of us push on the door until the realisation comes that the doorway to this heightened awareness doesn't push outward—it opens inward.'

I knew exactly what Wayne was talking about. How many people did I know who had described their lives just like that? They had learnt about new ways to be, but felt as if they just couldn't live it day to day. They were pushing against the door and wanting so much to step in. So what is the answer?

Practice generosity. People who give <u>willingly</u> of their possessions and their money are not doing it because they "have it to give". They are coming from a special heart space that is attracted to serving and sharing.

'You have to really learn to face a different way. I just finished writing a new book that I opened with the line, "We've been facing the wrong way!" Facing the wrong way means most of us have been looking outside of ourselves for something that will resolve the difficulties or struggles, or the things that seem to be missing in our lives, because we've been taught that's the way to do it.'

I drifted back from our conversation to Wayne's lecture. He was using a metaphor to explain how we search in the wrong places for solutions.

'I'm in my house and I drop my keys. The electricity has suddenly gone out, so it's dark and I can't see. In my wisdom I say, "Only a fool would look around in the dark for his keys". I notice that the street lights are on outside, so I go out there to stand under one to see if I can find

DYER STRAIGHT

Attempt to remove all enemies from your thoughts. The same intelligence that flows through you, flows through all human beings. When you know that you are connected to all, you cannot fathom striking out at others, let alone feeling hatred for them.

the keys I dropped. I search and search but can't find them. Suddenly, a friend shows up and helps me look for them for another half hour. Then he has an insight.

'"Where did you drop your keys, Wayne?" he asks. "What has that got to do with anything?" I reply. "Well, you might just think about where you dropped them," he says. "Well, I dropped them in the house, but it's dark in the house. I'm not going to look in the dark when I can look in the light for what I want," I answer.'

'It's an absurd image, isn't it, but that is exactly what we do when we have a problem in our lives. It is located inside, but we're looking for the solution to it out here. We want someone or something to change in order to be able to achieve this heightened, grand, miraculous state of awareness, yet it is available to each and every one of us!'

Demonstrate tolerance and love by ignoring what may have transpired in the past. Avoid the inclination to make someone wrong by pointing out the fallacies of their point of view with examples from their past. Let go of the desire to communicate.

Questions & Answers

∼ Let me take a moment to explain the journey I'm going to take you on. These pages list the answers to the most common questions asked of Wayne Dyer. They're not my questions: they're yours or those of your peers. To help you find answers easily, I've listed just the questions at the back of the book in the Index of Questions. In the text, I've placed the most frequently asked questions first, and you may find one of your questions answered here. I hope so. If not, by all means feel free to write to us at *The Planet Newspaper* and we'll make sure Wayne answers them—in the next book!

Lighten your material load, starting today. As you do so, less energy is spent hoarding, insuring, moving, polishing and so on. The less attached you are to your possessions, and the more you are able to share them with others unconditionally, the more peaceful your life will be.

What exactly is the Higher Self?

~ Sogyal Rinpoche said, 'Two people have been living in you all of your life. One is the ego: garrulous, demanding, hysterical and calculating. The other is your hidden spiritual being, whose still voice of wisdom you have rarely attended to'. That is your Higher Self.

How do we know if our Higher Self is prodding us to do something or whether it's just our ego?

~ The Higher Self pushes us towards more peace, joy and bliss in our lives; when we are operating from our Higher Self, we feel less competition and less

DYER
STRAIGHT

Allow your higher self to guide you when you have problems. Create a sentence that you repeat silently, such as: 'Please decide for me. I leave it in your hands'. This may seem like a cop-out, but I have found this technique helpful in many problem areas of my life.

separation from each other. But we don't really allow this part of ourselves to give us the sustenance, joy and capacity to be able to manifest miracles.

The ego believes strongly in competitiveness and comparing. It's always working against us. It is insane. Insanity is defined as something that is convincing you that you're something you're not. You are that which is eternal, changeless and disembodied, watching, observing, noticing, with no doubt. The ego is not something that you can really find—no-one's ever seen an ego.

Your ego is not yourself; it's just the idea you have of yourself. This idea is based on the fact that who you are is special. You will never get anywhere believing that. If you're special, then somebody else isn't. There's the assumption that God is playing favourites somehow,

Know that you are a soul with a body, rather than a body with a soul. Remember that your soul cannot be measured or observed with the tool that you use to view the material world.

and if we're all special, then what do we need a word like special for?

When we're in the ego we have this idea of ourselves that is somehow separate, unique, important and in competition with others. We feel that anything that might offend us, or anything we don't like, or anyone out there who doesn't fit in with how we want them to be is something that we have to defend ourselves against. We literally grow up trying to play this ego game; having to defend ourselves and prove that we're right and making ourselves feel important.

We have all these incredible attachments to labels that we place on ourselves. I think that reaching that higher awareness is really like a disappearing act. If you want to reach this higher state of awareness, you have to give up your primary identification with any label you might have.

*You have a very
powerful mind that can
make anything happen
as long as you keep
yourself centred.*

You have to abandon the labels and understand this fundamental truth: that we are not human beings having a spiritual experience, but spiritual beings having a human experience. The quality of your human experience has absolutely nothing to do with this form that you showed up in, with this garage that you have parked your soul in for a while.

What are the benefits of letting go of the ego?

◈ You can get beyond this whole stage of just surviving! You can get to a really higher place where you begin to literally manage the coincidences of your life and create an energy about yourself where you can attract to you whatever it is that you need. You can always be in the right place at the right time.

DYER STRAIGHT

*When you live on
a round planet, there's
no choosing sides.*

Is there a guiding force in our lives?

~ I see everything that shows up in my life as Divine. Everything and everyone is sent to me by this Divine Organising Intelligence that has many names. I don't care what you call it, whether you want to call it God, or Soul, or Spirit, or Consciousness, or the Universal Tao or Louise! What we call it is not relevant, but it is a very powerful force that is in us and there are ways to have a primary identification with it.

Can this force help us get to that heightened state of awareness?

~ The Divine Organising Intelligence can be awakened and put to use, and it

DYER STRAIGHT

*What distinguishes
what's alive from what is
dead is growth, be it in
plants or in you.*

doesn't have to be something you *believe* in. Most of us know about God, but I'm talking about something radically different than knowing *about* it: I'm talking about knowing *it*.

How long does it take to become enlightened?

~ Most of us in the West have come to believe that to be enlightened, to be successful, one would have to follow a prescribed set of rules and dogma handed to us by others. People believe they need to set goals, struggle, sacrifice, get proper training, find someone who knows more than they do, do an apprenticeship and ultimately reach this place called enlightenment or success, whatever you want to call it. But this takes a long time and sometimes we get there and its over. Of course, it's quite OK to do it this way, but

Remember that what you think about expands. Since you have the power to make your inner world work for you or against you, use it to create the images of bliss that you want to occur in your material world. Eventually, that inner bliss will be the blueprint that you consult as the architect of your everyday life.

if you read Eastern philosophy and become engrossed in the power of the mind and power of intelligence, you will see that the Eastern masters have discovered another way. The Japanese call it *sartori*. This means instant awakening—gaining an understanding of something in the click of the fingers that can change our lives forever. Most of us have experienced *sartori*. Think back to those times when you have experienced significant and dramatic changes in your life in one instant, and then walked away knowing your life has changed.

How do we make the transition from looking outside for solutions, to finding them within?

~ We have to learn how to have an inner candle flame that never flickers,

DYER
STRAIGHT

Get a clear picture in your mind of something that you would like to see happen in your life: a job opportunity, a new love, quitting an addictive behaviour, or whatever. Keep your inner focus on this picture, and extend love outwardly with this picture in mind. The results will be worth your effort.

even when the worst goes before us. We have to learn to surrender and let go of our attachment to the results and understand that our purpose has nothing to do with the outcome; it has to do with focusing on the process and letting God take care of that process. We don't realise that life is what is happening to us while we're busy making other plans; we're constantly trying to shift our attention outward and be somewhere else.

What are the keys to gaining heightened awareness?

~ *The first key* to heightened awareness is erasing your past. If you don't have a story, then you don't have to live up to it. Just let go of your story and all of your primary identifications! Begin to erase that

Be cognisant of the fact that everyone who comes into your life in any capacity is valuable. The petty tyrants are just as divine as those who provided you with encouragement and support. Those whom we judge to be unfortunate or evil can teach us our greatest lessons.

part of yourself that you used to think of as who you are and begin to see yourself as something very different than just this physical being that showed up here.

There are four major categories of life: minerals, vegetables, animals and humans. Look at these four things: a rock, a tomato plant, a jaguar and a person. What is it that differentiates them? If you ground them all up, put them together in a bag and sent them off to the lab for a chemical analysis, you wouldn't be able to tell one from the other. Everything on this planet is made up of the same raw material—we are all made up of the same stuff!

The Divine Organising Intelligence has taken all the raw material and arranged it into different accumulations of stuff, so what separates us from the others is not the raw material, its *awareness*.

Remind yourself that God created you in perfect love that is changeless and eternal. Your body is changing, as is your mind, so you are not that body or that mind. You were created as a spirit that is pure love. That is where you want to keep your attention focused.

We look at a rock and say it has limited awareness because it just sits there. It doesn't know enough to come out of the rain. A tomato plant has a little more awareness; it produces offspring and moves towards the sunlight, which rocks can't do. But it's not attached to its offspring. Because we're writing the rules, we say it has less awareness. If tomato plants were writing the rules they'd probably think we were really weird because the tomato plant just has babies and says, 'Here, eat my babies. Make marinara sauce out of my babies; I have no problem with that'. But if you took a jaguar's babies and tried to do the same thing, you'd get a very different reaction.

Then there's us. And the problem with us is that we live our lives at the same level of awareness as animals. We seem content to be in survival mode. We never

Spend special moments in awe of the miracle that life truly is. Awe is the loving appreciation of God's work and the presence of the Divine Intelligence.

think of ourselves as having a higher level of awareness that is beyond just surviving. We hold onto our beliefs and carry them with us wherever we go.

But if you feel that you want to change anything about your life or create something for yourself, you can. If you can conceive it, you can create it—whatever it is. You have the capacity to manifest, but you can't do it the way you've been taught! You really have to get rid of your story!

There are seven little words that are the key to the universe: 'As you think so shall you be'. Once you know that, what you think about expands; then you become very careful about what you think about, because *the ancestor to every action is a thought.* The corollary of all this is: if you can't *conceive* of it you can't *create* it, and that is the problem. We mostly can't conceive of awareness because we think we are this

Instead of cursing the past, bless it and forgive yourself entirely. When you know that all of those experiences were a part of the Divine Design of your life, you can afford to forgive.

body we showed up in and our primary identification is with this thing that we carry with us wherever we go.

I really believe that when you start to let go of your past, you make a divine connection and begin to attract to you that which you need. You think that it's just coincidence, but it happens to everybody. Carl Jung called it *synchronicity*. Everyone has had experiences with synchronicity. It's like a collaboration with fate: you have a thought and what you thought of begins to show up. Synchronicity particularly happens when we're not trying to force it to happen. We should just let go and allow synchronicity to happen in our lives for us, but instead we say, 'Well it happened before, so I'm going to work even harder at it'. When you work harder, you start to push, and when you start to push,

Be aware of your thoughts, and remind yourself that the simple act of thinking is evidence that there is an invisible energy that flows through you at all times.

you're starting to tell God how to do it and it doesn't work for you.

What's the difference between setting a goal or knowing what you want to happen in your life, and pushing against the force?

～ We don't need to push for it to happen, we only need to have *intention*. When you have the intention to create something in your life, it begins to show up, which leads us to **the second key** to higher awareness, which I call *banishing the doubt*. You can do this really well already in your dream state. You don't have any doubt in your dreams that you can do something. Shakespeare said, 'Our

Try on the concept that beliefs restrict you, while knowings empower you. A belief is merely a mental note attached to your lapel by your mommy. A knowing is etched into the cells of your being, and therefore lives within you with an absence of doubt.

doubts are our traitors'. William Blake said, 'If the sun and moon should ever doubt, they would immediately go out'. The same is true for you.

For one third of your life you are in this dream state. I ask people, 'When you dream, where's the bed? What happens to it for eight hours?' The bed is just a symbol of everything you leave behind. If in your dream there are some flowers on the other side of the room and you want to look at them more closely, you just bring them to you. And when you don't want them any more you simply send them away. When you want your grandmother, even though she's been dead for twenty years, there she is. If you need to be fourteen again, you're fourteen again.

If you need to be married to a jerk for twenty years in your dream, you just say,

Get back to nature. Give yourself time in the woods, trekking in the mountains, walking in open meadow, or walking barefoot on the beach.

'Thank you very much for showing up! I needed an asshole at this point and now you're here'. You don't get mad at the jerk for showing up; you realise that you just bring to you everything you need for the dream. Then you get to waking consciousness and suddenly you think that you're no longer in a dream—and that's the illusion.

Samuel Taylor Coleridge tested our boundaries of belief when he wrote:

> *What if you slept, and what if in your sleep you dreamed,*
> *and what if in your dream you went to heaven*
> *and there picked a strange and wonderful flower,*
> *and what if when you woke, you held that flower in your hand,*
> *ah, what then?*

Make a daily effort to look upon others without condemnation. Every judgement takes you away from your goal of peace. Keep in mind that you do not define anyone with your judgement; you only define yourself as someone who needs to judge.

The quality of the human experience you are having is dependent not upon this physical form you showed up in, but on something much more powerful. There is a place *beyond* the physical. This body we all showed up in is just our curriculum to God. It's all in order, just the way it is supposed to be.

Is there more to us than this physical body?

∾ There was a time before you were here in this form of yours. There was an instant when you were nowhere, just before your conception. We all got to be here the same way. Whether you like it or not, we all went on a picnic with our father and came home with our mother. You go on the picnic, now you're in *nowhere*. You

Be conscious of your thoughts, of the make-up of your internal dialogue. Know that any thoughts you repeat that are contrary to your Divine eternal essence are keeping you from experiencing the joyous and complete life you deserve.

go on the picnic and you're in *now here*. It's all the same. And where do you think you're going? Back to nowhere. When you take complete responsibility for all of it; become the observer and begin to let go of everything, you take on a different dimension of being.

There is an intelligence and you are a part of this in this parenthesis in eternity which is your life. Everything you needed for this physical journey is handed to you. But there's also another journey—a divine, formless, unbounded intelligence that flows through you and watches you doing the things you do. I know strange and wonderful things have happened to my form since I showed up here. But it doesn't bother me; I become the observer. The person who is doing the watching, that Divine Invisible, is not aging at all. It is ageless, timeless, and

Develop the ability to witness your thoughts by stepping back and watching them enter and exit your mind. Just observing the flow of thoughts will slow the mind down to the still point where you can experience God.

formless and you must know that. You can't see it or get hold of it, yet it is controlling everything.

There is a song I love by Jackson Browne called *For A Dancer* in which he says: 'go on ahead and throw some seeds of your own'. To me, this means transcending your past and creating your own reality.

That is such powerful thinking. In order to be able to reach this heightened level of awareness where we can create the miracles we want, we have to transcend the thinking of the dancer and become the choreographer, dancer *and* producer of our own life. We don't do it because we get stuck in survival mode, and no one ever comes along and says, 'Of course you can create miracles and heal yourself! Certainly you have the capacity to bring love into your life! Of course we can make the world better!'

Become aware that there are no accidents in our intelligent universe. Realise that everything that shows up in your life has something to teach you. Appreciate everyone and everything in your life.

People ask me if they can win the lottery with this kind of attitude. I say, 'I don't know, but how would you feel if you won the lottery?' Some say they would feel very secure, safe and blissful. I say, 'Well I can help you with that. The only illusion you have is that you have to have a lottery to be able to feel like that. You don't have to have something like a lottery to experience that kind of bliss'. Being a dancer really means listening to what *other* people have choreographed for us. Being a producer means choreographing it for ourselves.

With God, all things are possible. What does that leave out? It leaves out nothing! If you have a knowing within you that you can divinely create things in your life and you don't let anyone in your life smear that picture, you know that if you can conceive of it, you can

*Anything that keeps
you from growing is never
worth defending.*

manifest it. You can begin, through the power of intention, to manage these coincidences of your life and create whatever it is that you need.

How can we move things from just being ideas into being our reality?

∾ You can move something from an idea into a reality by placing your attention somewhere and refusing to be distracted from it. When you place your attention somewhere, you are acting out that saying: 'as you think, so shall you be'.

The ancestor to every action in your life is nothing more than a reflection of where you have been placing your attention. It has nothing to do with the circumstances of your life. As James Allen

If you think the solution is outside of yourself, but the problem is inside of yourself, then you're living an illusion. The fact is that every problem is in your mind, and so is every solution.

pointed out at the beginning of the century, 'Circumstances don't make a man, they reveal him'. The people who are in the worst of circumstances are the ones who need to hear this message the most. If you want to transcend your circumstances you have to challenge the kind of thinking that has brought the circumstances into your life.

How do we erase our past?

~ If you want to erase your past, you have to give up the idea that those things which have happened to you in your life that you don't like are really not part of the divineness of it all. Our lesson is to go beyond form and into transformation.

We have an energy body as well as a physical body. It's an etheric body that's with us at all times. It's like an invisible

Know that there is an invisible intelligence in everything. You have the power to make contact with this Divine Intelligence and create a life of bliss.

shield of energy that surrounds us. It determines our perceptions of reality and it is only through being able to shift this energy that you can have clarity and begin to see like you've never seen before. We each have the capacity to shift our energy in terms of our own lives as well as that around us. It was said that when Buddha or Jesus would go into a village, just their presence would raise the consciousness of the people in that village.

You have the capacity to be able to communicate telepathically with anyone on this planet and communicate with those who have left before, because that which is real is that which never changes, and that which was never born, never dies. Each and every one of you is trapped inside something that is constantly changing, but there's a part of you that isn't.

~

Forgiveness is the most powerful thing you can do to get on the spiritual path. If you can't do it, you can forget about getting to higher levels of awareness and creating real magic in your life.

You also have the capacity to be able to heal. Whatever universal law that has ever allowed any miracle to ever transpire on the history of this planet is still on the books. It's just a matter of learning how to tune into it. You have to start to rely on your powerful energy body and shift your energy outward. Next you must banish all doubt and open up to the possibility that you are unlimited in the dimension of the formless and in the place in you which has no form.

We're all just physical manifestations of the same essence. That's all we are. When you make your primary identification with that which is watching, that which is the commander, you begin to have a whole new awareness—a knowing. And with that knowing you can project outward and create anything in your life.

The whole universal system is held together through love, harmony and cooperation. If you use your thoughts according to these principles you can transcend anything that gets in the way.

I sometimes experience doubt about my ability to create the things I really want in my life. How do I overcome this?

∾ If you experience doubt about *anything* in your life, that doubt is what you'll act on. What you think about is what expands. Once you know this you start to acknowledge this invisible observer who watches this body go through these motions. You transcend the big lie which suggests there are certain things you can do and things you can't. Everything you know comes from within. Everything you believe is an intellectual act. Everything you know is a metaphysical, cellular act. Shift to

~

If you take two sentences out of your life: "I'm tired," and "I don't feel well," you will have cured about 50 percent of your tiredness and your illness.

~

knowings. We then have beliefs that have become so strong they are knowings now. You can't know from instruction: I hear and I forget, I see and I remember, I do and I understand.

The knowing is metaphysical. Once you get it, it stays with you. Knowing will never let you down—beliefs will always let you down. When you have a knowing, don't allow anyone else to smudge it in any way.

To get past doubt you must begin to understand the difference between what it is that you believe and what it is that you *know*. Everything you believe was handed to you by someone or something outside of yourself and therefore it comes attached with doubt. Knowing is a metaphysical experience. In order to have a knowing, you have to rid yourself of all aspects of doubt.

~

*In order to make a
visualisation a reality in the
world of form, you must be
willing to do whatever
it takes to make it happen.*

~

How come when I feel like I'm really achieving growth in my life, something negative comes along and knocks me back down?

~ The Kabbala says that not only do you need to have a certain amount of energy to be able to generate a shift in energy, but in order to generate that energy, you must first fall. You must experience a fall in order to generate an energy to move from one level to the next on this planet. That's how it works. You go down to get up.

Every fall you have experienced in your life has been nothing more than the way God has said, 'Here's how I get your attention'. What do you think a divorce,

DYER STRAIGHT

*If you build a house
that has as its foundation
only one support system
and that particular
support collapses,
your entire house
will topple.*

breakup, accident or illness is about? The ego is very protective about you having a crisis because when you have a crisis you find God, and the ego is terrified of God. The ego is terrified of your finding the higher place within you that will transcend virtually anything that you call a problem.

When did you first find the strength to move forward?

~ It was in a moment of prayer years and years ago. I was on my knees and God said to me, 'Wayne, you've tried everything else, now try me'. And it was done. Instant awakening! I turned my higher power into the blessing that it is, instead of relying on the ego. When you go there and find that place you'll begin to see that every transcendent move in your life generally was preceded by some kind of fall.

Blame is a neat little device that you can use whenever you don't want to take responsibility for something in your life. Use it and you will avoid all risks and impede your own growth.

How can we turn challenges into opportunities?

∼ When something negative is happening instead of asking, 'How could this be happening to me?' say to yourself, 'There's probably a real lesson in this. I'm going to detach myself and observe it, and as I notice it, I'm not identifying with it, it's not me. This is not my body. I am not my body. I am that which is observing. I know that whatever I'm going through is in Divine Order'.

What we have to do is transcend the paradigms that we have in our life. A paradigm is a way of thinking that we're stuck in. I get up every day at 4 am. I decided I wanted to challenge a paradigm in my life—the paradigm that I have to have a certain amount of sleep in order for me to have a good day or to have the

The only difference between someone who's beautiful and unattractive is a judgement. There's nobody in the world who is unattractive. No one on this planet. Unattractive is just what people decide to believe.

energy to get through the day. I said to myself, 'instead of sleeping eight hours a day I'm going to see if I can get it down to four and still have the same energy'.

We sleep at the wrong time. We sleep when we could be talking to God, when it's silent and peaceful and our brain is ready to receive and hear what we need to hear. We're awake at the time when we're most groggy and sleepy. If you spent two or three hours every morning of your life walking in silence along the rivers, in your backyard—anywhere—your life would change. The ideas that have come to me in those moments have been incredible. And guess what, I don't get tired! If I get a bit sleepy at three o'clock in the afternoon, I just meditate for ten minutes and I'm fine again.

It's very hard for us to get out of paradigms. In 1967 Mother Theresa was

Deficiency-motivated people spend their lives in the disease called more—always trying to acquire something to make themselves feel complete and to repair the deficiency.

asked if she would march against the Vietnam War. She said, 'No, I will not. But if you have a march for peace I'll be there!' There's a big difference between being *against* war and being *for* peace. It takes a paradigm shift. What you are for empowers you. What you are against weakens you. So the paradigm shift is to be *for* something.

Instead of looking at what you don't like about someone, think about what you *do* like, and what you think about will expand. When you first meet someone and fall in love you don't say, 'You know, if you were just a bit taller I'd be crazy about you'.

Why can't I create miracles in my life?

~ Your life is the product of the choices you have been making up until now. Think

~

*Children need to know
that the words
"It's impossible" are not a
part of your vocabulary
and that you are a supporter
of their dreams.*

of your life as a ship heading up the river. The ship represents your body. As it's moving ahead, you're able to stand at the stern and look down into the water and see its wake. What is the wake? It's the trail left behind by the ship's movement. What is driving the ship? The *present moment energy* that is being generated by the engine of the ship. Is it possible for the wake to drive the ship? No. The wake cannot drive the ship.

But is this happening in your life? Most of us live this illusion that our wake (our past) is driving the ship. That is, the things that happened to us when we were younger are making us go in our present direction. You can hardly sit through a conversation in which you won't hear someone who has bought into this illusion. But it's not true. What *is* driving the ship of your life is whatever present moment decisions you are generating *in this instant*. If you think

*Detachment is the
absence of a need to hold on
to anyone or anything.
It is a way of thinking
and being which gives
us the freedom to flow
with life. Detachment is the
only vehicle available
to take you from striving to
arriving.*

your past is driving the ship of your life, you cannot get to a heightened level of awareness. In reality, your past has nothing to do with the way you are today. It's just the trail you've left behind.

We all have this bag of manure that we smear all over us and then wonder why our life smells bad. You've got to drop that baggage and let go of this insane idea that the wake is driving the ship of your life. You have to understand that the parents you have or had did what they had to do given the conditions of their life. You can't ask any more than that. Mark Twain said, 'Forgiveness is the fragrance that the violet sheds on the heel that has crushed it'.

Surrender. Stop the struggle; stop the fight; let go of the goals of where you want to be and where you're headed. Someone once said, 'If you want to make

*Be a student.
Stay open and willing to
learn from everyone and
anyone. Being a student
means you have room
for new input.*

God laugh, tell her your plans'. There is something inside of you that will allow you to do what you want to do. Suspend your disbelief: banish the doubt. Whatever it is you need to know will come to you in meditation if you stay on purpose and allow the inner to guide you. Your prayer is talking to God. Your intuition is *God* talking to *you*.

I want to make the transition, but I keep hearing negatives in my head every time I try to stretch my awareness. How do I stop this?

The third key to higher awareness is shutting down the inner dialogue. The inner

In regard to addictions, when you are pursuing poisons, you can never get enough of what you don't want. You become what you think about all day long and those days eventually become your lifetime.

dialogue is this constant chatter that's always going on in your mind, and it's just a repetition of all the beliefs you've had handed to you by other people.

Your mind is like a pond, and the surface of the pond is where all the disturbances are. If you had a pebble and dropped it, you could see it dropping from chatter to quiet. Usually it goes beneath the surface which is what I call analysis. This is the intellectual violence where we pick apart our thoughts. Analysis is anal retentive.

The pebble goes below analysis to synthesis, where instead of seeing how things are torn apart, you see how things are held together. Ultimately, the pebble goes further until it begins to quiet the mind and finally it reaches the place where you empty the mind. The pebble comes to rest in this place which we call

*The winning attitude
is one that allows you to
think of yourself as a
winner all the time
while still giving yourself
room to grow.*

'the unified field of all possibilities'. The poet Rumi wrote:

> *Out beyond all ideas of right doing and wrong doing, there is a field.*
> *I'll meet you there.*
> *You can meet your love there.*

I seem to get so caught up in my emotions. How can I stop this?

~ The fourth key to higher awareness is *cultivating the witness*. This is where you begin to see that you are much more than your troubles. You are the witness, the observer. Your lower self is abandoned when you cultivate your witness. You can witness your body and your thoughts. You can watch yourself be angry in one moment and blissful in the

True joy and the exhilarating feeling of being at peace with yourself and the world comes to the person who lets his or her physical world flow from the pleadings of the soul.

next all over the same thing. You have to let go of your primary identification with this body and become the noticer and know that where you place your attention in a quantum physical sense is what you will manifest. As you get good at it you begin to place your attention only on that which you want to manifest.

I know you can go from poverty, from an alcoholic background, from hunger or from having no parents around to a life of abundance, prosperity and fulfilment. I know it! Not because I've read about it or because someone else has told me about it, but because that has been my past. The same thing is true of your experience with God. You can know God by being quiet, being silent, by cultivating the witness, banishing the doubt and finally, by taming the ego. The ego is that part of you which is attached to

> As you become awakened, you're not ego-defined anymore. You're not defined by what you get and how you get it. You're more defined by "I can be internally more at peace" and "How can I help other people do that?"

your separateness and doesn't allow you to think of yourself as connected to all.

Everyone is on their own path and doing exactly what they are supposed to be doing. There are no accidents. For example, you may be with someone who is not only not on your path, but is not even on an *entrance ramp* to your path. But you signed up for it! If you don't want them in your life ask yourself, 'Why did I attract him/her?', instead of, 'Why does he/she keep showing up?'. Begin to see that you create it all. Once you have done that, you can then open up an energy chakra within you that removes some of this negative energy that you've accumulated over a lifetime of doubting and dancing to the tune that others have been playing for you.

As Robert Frost says: 'Inside of you, we all sit around in a ring and suppose, while

You can't get prune juice from an orange, no matter how hard you squeeze it. You can't give hate if you only have love inside.

the secret sits in the centre and knows'. That's who you are. *The secret in the centre that knows.* The keys to higher awareness are very simply erasing your past, getting rid of your story, banishing all doubt, cultivating the witness, getting silent, knowing God and taming the ego. It's that simple, believe me!

~ In Gifts From Eykis, *Dr Dyer again furnishes his readers with many interesting points to ponder on. He provokes readers to wonder at the human species and many of the attitudes that are ingrained in our cultures.*

It chronicles an exchange arrangement between an earthling and a citizen from outer space. Dr Dyer uses the parable format effectively, entertaining readers but enabling them ultimately to look inward to their own thoughts and actions.

Once again, the bestselling author of Your Erroneous Zones *and* Real Magic *teaches: 'There us no way to happiness, happiness is the way!'.*

*Did you ever notice
how difficult it is to argue
with someone who is
not obsessed with
being right?*

Why did you choose Uranus as Eykis' planet?

~ Before I wrote the book I used to say jokingly, 'If you want to be happy, get your head out of Uranus', and I used to use that all the time, so it just worked. Originally, instead of *Gifts from Eykis*, I was going to call it *Get Your Head Out of Uranus*. In actual fact, it really came from a very spiritual book called *The Urancha Book* which I read from fairly frequently and Uranus just seemed to be the place. That was the only reason, there was nothing magical about it.

What's the main difference between Uranus & Earth in the book?

~ The main difference in the novel is that the people on Uranus have a reason

~

Abundance is about looking at life and knowing that we have everything we need for complete happiness, and then being able to celebrate each and every moment of life.

~

to be neurotic—it's built into their reality—and on earth, people choose to be neurotic. There's nothing about our planet that requires people to be neurotic, whereas on Uranus it is required, as anxiety really does attack, for example. For instance, they report an anxiety attack on the weather report. Eykis was the woman on the weather report who gave the anxiety attack report warning her listeners not only to watch out for snow storms and all that, but also anxiety. The whole premise of this terrible place is that people are neurotic because they have to be, because there's nothing they can do about it. Guilt serves a purpose: the characters get to go into rewind and redo things and so on. That's why Eykis came to earth—to figure out why people would ever *choose* to be neurotic.

Rulers can remove our outer places of worship, but the inner place, that invisible corner of freedom that is ever present in each of us, can never be legislated.

Is this your first and only novel?

~ Well, I wrote a novel when I was a teenager, but this is the first one published.

Why did you decide to write in the fictional mode?

~ It was just another vehicle—another way to get my message across. I had already written five books at that time and I just decided that I wanted to tell a story and that I wanted to add some humour and satire to it. I've always felt that parables were very effective ways to reach people. *Gulliver's Travels* and other books demonstrate that. Through a story and through the characters in a story you can express more and attract many people who don't read non-fiction.

*Give up the "want".
Know in your heart that
you do not need one more
thing to make yourself
complete, and then watch
all those external
things become less and
less significant in
your heart.*

What books are you working on currently?

~ I've just finished writing two books that will be published next year. One of them is called *Manifesting Your Destiny - The Nine Spiritual Principles for Getting Everything you Want*. It's about connecting to the Divine Source in all things, and understanding that we all have the capacity to attract to us what we need and want for ourselves, and that it's not a power that is restricted to just a few people. As I have mentioned before, one of the things that Jesus said was, 'Even the least among you can do all that I have done and even greater things'. Most of us have disempowered ourselves. We don't really believe that we have the power to attract to us what we want or to manifest whatever our

You don't get abused because there are a lot of abusers out there. You get abused because you send out signals that say, "Abuse me. I'll take that".

hearts desire. What I've done is to write down nine principles that I just allowed to come to me. When you follow these principles that I have followed in my life, you can get what you desire.

The other book which will be released is called *A Promise Is A Promise*. It's the story of a mother whose daughter has been in a coma for 27 years, and she has taken care of her the whole time. She has fed her every two hours for 27 years, 24 hours a day, and has taken her blood every four hours. She also turns her every two hours, and is just totally committed. It's the first real story of unconditional love that I've ever seen. She's like a modern-day Mother Theresa in the United States, and she's tremendously in debt. I was so moved by her story that I decided to write this book and donate all the royalties and all of the profits to keep

~

*We are our form and
our formlessness.
We are both visible and
invisible, and we need to
honour our totality,
not just what we
can see and touch.*

~

her out of debt. The last thing her daughter said to her when she was 16 years old in 1970, January 3rd, was 'You won't leave me will you mommy, you won't leave me?' And the mother came and said 'I won't leave you, I promise, and a promise is a promise'.

~ *Many of Wayne's devoted followers wrote in with questions about Wayne the man. They want to know how such a spiritual person lives in real life, and how he copes with being so much in demand. They also wanted to hear about his family, so I closed my question-and-answer sessions with a few personal questions.*

However, I barely had time. Readers will recall that in the preface I mentioned that Wayne's limousine had gone to the wrong location and that Wayne and I had to jog back to the hotel to find the limousine which was to take him to the airport. The following questions and answers are the product of the conversation we had while dodging passers-by,

Only a ghost wallows around in his past, explaining himself with descriptors based on a life already lived. You are what you choose today, not what you've chosen before.

crossing the road and avoiding being run over. Consequently the answers are not elaborate but short and to the point. I've even cut out all my puffing and panting from between the questions.

Wayne, do you like touring?

～ I love touring. I wouldn't do it for any other reason. I certainly don't need to. I love speaking and I love writing, and in order to speak you have to travel, unless you want to talk to the same people every night. It just goes with the territory. I speak internationally a lot now. In the last year I spoke in Europe on several occasions, as well as in Singapore, Kuala Lumpur, South America, Peru and Argentina. I have been invited to speak in South Africa next year. It's like a worldwide revolution, and I just go where I'm sent.

To be attached to your physical appearance is to ensure a lifetime of suffering as you watch your form go through the natural motions that began the moment of your conception.

On average, how many cities would you visit in a year?

~ Oh, about fifty.

How many children do you have?

~ We have eight: six daughters and two sons.

What music do you listen to when you relax?

~ Mozart and Jackson Browne.

If you are still following a career path that you decided upon as a young person, ask yourself this questions today: Would I seek out the advice of a teenager for vocational guidance?

When you're at home and you get a chance to cook, what dish are you really proud of?

~ I don't do much cooking, but my vegie burgers have acquired a certain reputation.

Who do you most admire in your field?

~ I admire everyone who's out there teaching. I have some dear friends whose work I admire. They include Louise Hay, Deepak Chopra, Stuart Wilde, Marianne Williamson and Dennis Waitley.

By concentrating on your breathing, by meditation, and by affirming aloud your intentions, you can re-energise yourself on your life's journey.

If you could invite six people from any time in history to join you in a dinner party, who would they be?

~ Buddha, Jesus, Ghandi, Hitler, Stalin and Alexander the Great.

Where did the title the 'Father of Motivation' come from?

~ I'm the father of Shane, Stephanie, Skye, Sommer, Serena, Sands, Saje and Tracy. I might as well be the father of motivation too as long as there's no paternity suits involved.

At this point Wayne had his hands around my neck, saying, 'Leon if I don't get

~

You, a person with a vision, are like a pebble in a stream, moving ever outward to infinity, impacting on all who come into contact with the ripple.

~

to the airport, my wife is going to kill me because I won't be home for Thanksgiving'.

'But Wayne, I've still got a pocketful of questions!' I moan.

'Leon, leave it for the next book' he said as he walks towards the gates at the airport.

'OK, OK' I concede. 'But just one last question. If you're the *Father of Motivation*, who's the mother?'

*We send our kids off
to school to major in
"labelling" and think
the ones who do it best
deserve the highest grades.*

About the Author - Leon Nacson

∽ LEON NACSON was born in Alexandria, Egypt, to Greek parents. In 1952 he migrated to Australia where he founded *The Planet* newspaper, a well-established publication that deals with environmental, health and personal development issues. He is also the Managing Director of Nacson Promotions International, a visionary company that has facilitated seminars and workshops throughout Australia for such notable individuals as Deepak Chopra, Louise Hay, Shakti Gawain, Stuart Wilde and Denise Linn. Nacson Promotions also publishes books on health and personal growth. The company has over ten best-sellers to its credit.

*A heart starts beating
in a mother's womb six
weeks after conception
and life as we observe
it is under way.
It remains a mystery
to all of the greatest
minds on the planet*

Having published so many other authors, In 1993 Leon felt inspired to write his first book, *A Dreamer's Guide to the Galaxy*, on dreams and dreaming. In it, he synthesised much of the knowledge he had gleaned over the years, and showed readers how to 'wake' up to themselves. Leon followed this book with three more: *Aromatherapy for Lovers and Dreamers*, *Stars, Cards and Dreams* and *Aromatherapy for Meditation and Contemplation.*

DYER
STRAIGHT

You mustn't attempt to will anything. You need only be willing. Even though the sky will be different in a few hours, its present perfection and completeness is not deficient. You, too, are presently perfect and not deficient because you will be different tomorrow.

About Wayne Dyer

∼ DR WAYNE W. DYER is one of the most widely read, internationally renowned authors in the field of self-development today. He has written many bestselling books (*Everyday Wisdom*, *Your Erroneous Zones*, *Real Magic* and *Your Sacred Self*), is featured in a number of audio and video tapes, and has appeared on over 5,200 television and radio programs.

*To enter the realm of
real magic you will have
to suspend all thoughts of
limitation and become
a spiritual being first,
a being who has no
limitation in your inner
domain where bound-
arise are non-existent.*

Other books by Leon Nacson

- A Dreamers Guide to the Galaxy
- Aromatherapy for Lovers & Dreamers
  co-authored by Karen Downes and Judith White
- Stars, Cards and Dreams
  co-authored by Matthew Favaloro
- Aromatherapy for Meditation & Contemplation
  co-authored by Karen Downes and Judith White

Acting as if you were already what you want to become and knowing that you can become it is the way to remove self-doubt and enter your real-magic kingdom.

Other Publications from Wayne Dyer

BOOKS

- Everyday Wisdom
- Gifts From Eykis
- No More Holiday Blues
- 101 Ways to Transform Your Life
- Pulling Your Own Strings
- Real Magic
- The Sky's the Limit
- Staying on the Path
- What Do You Really Want For Your Children?
- You'll See It When You Believe It
- Your Erroneous Zones
- Your Sacred Self

*Have in your mind
that which could constitute
a miracle for you. Get the
vision. Suspend disbelief
and scepticism. Allow
yourself to take
the journey toward
real magic.*

AUDIOS

- Choosing Your Own Greatness
- Everyday Wisdom (book-on-tape)
- Freedom Through Higher Awareness
- How to Be a No-Limit Person
- The Keys to Higher Awareness Transformation
- The Universe Within You

VIDEOS

- Creating Real Magic in Your Life

CALANDERS

- Everyday Wisdom Engagement Calender
- Everyday Wisdom Flip Calender

We talk privately to God and call it prayer. So why does a return call seem so far-fetched, particularly if we believe that there is some universal intelligence out there that we are addressing?

Index of Questions

- What exactly is the *Higher Self*? 1

- How do we know if our *Higher Self* is prodding us to do something or whether it's just *our ego*? 1

- What are the benefits of *letting go of the ego*? 7

- Is there a *guiding force* in our lives? 9

- Can this force help us get to that *heightened* state of *awareness*? 9

- How long does it take to *become enlightened*? 11

- How do we make the transition from looking outside for *solutions*, to finding them *within*? 13

DYER
STRAIGHT

Treasure your physical being as a vehicle that houses your soul. Once you have the inner way, the outer way will follow.

- What are the keys to gaining *heightened awareness*? 14

- What's the difference between *setting a goal* or knowing what you want to happen in your life, and pushing against the force? 25

- Is there more to us than this *physical body*? 31

- How can we move things from just being ideas into being *our reality*? 39

- How do we *erase our past*? 41

- I sometimes experience doubt about my *ability to create* the things I really want in my life. How do I overcome this? 47

- How come when I feel like I'm really *achieving growth* in my life, something negative comes along and knocks me back down? 51

~

Forgiveness is man's highest achievement because it shows true enlightenment in action. It shows that one is in touch with the energy of love.

~

- When did you first find the *strength* to move *forward*? 53
- How can we turn *challenges* into *opportunities*? 55
- Why can't I *create miracles* in my life? 59
- I want to *make the transition*, but I keep hearing negatives in my head every time I try to stretch my awareness. How do I stop this? 65
- I seem to get so caught up in my *emotions*. How can I stop this? 69
- Why did you choose Uranus as *Eykis'* planet? 77
- What's the main difference between *Uranus & Earth* in the book? 77
- Is this your *first* and only *novel*? .. 81
- Why did you decide to write in the *fictional mode*? 81

Let go of any repetitious inner dialogue about the horrors and tragedies of the world. Know that everything that happens is perfect, even the parts that you dislike. All of your opinions about how things should take place are nothing more than notions you have of how God should be orchestrating this play.

- What *books* are you working on *currently*? 83
- Wayne, do you like *touring*? 89
- On average, how *many cities* would you visit in a year? 91
- How many *children* do you have? 91
- What *music* do you listen to when you relax? 91
- When you're at home and you get a *chance to cook*, what dish are you really proud of? 93
- Who do you most *admire* in your field? 93
- If you could invite six people from any time in *history* to join you in *a dinner party*, who would they be? 95
- Where did the title the *'Father of Motivation'* come? 95